Money God's Way

Rich Or Poor It's Up To You

BY
SPENCER COFFMAN

Money God's Way

While every precaution has been taken in the preparation of this book, the author and/or publisher assumes no responsibility for errors or omissions, or for damages resulting from the use of the information contained herein.

Money God's Way: Rich or Poor It's Up To You

First edition. June 2020.

ISBN: 979-8-6523282-8-3 (Paperback)
ISBN: 978-1-3869087-2-2 (Digital)

Copyright © 2018, 2020 by Spencer Coffman.
Cover Design by Spencer Coffman
All Rights Reserved.

Written by Spencer Coffman.
SpencerCoffman.com

Money God's Way

Money God's Way

ALSO BY SPENCER COFFMAN

A Guide To Deception
Relax And Unwind
Work Less Live More
A Healthier You!
Affiliate Marketing Expert
More Facebook Everything
365 Days Of Devotion For Everyone
YouTube Takeover
Find Us On Pinterest
Start Affiliate Marketing
Deception Tips Revised & Expanded
The Twelve Apostles
The End-Times Prophecy
Two Sets Of Ten

Money God's Way

Money God's Way

Money God's Way

INTRODUCTION

The topic of money is a touchy subject when it comes to Christians. This is because the majority of people don't understand money. In addition, the majority of Christians don't understand what God says about money. This is amazing because money and possessions are the second most talked about thing in the Bible. That mean, if people don't understand what God says about money then they must not be reading their Bibles.

This is a very sad realization. But wait, it gets even sadder. The average American household owns four Bibles, yet only one-fifth of Americans regularly read their Bible. This is why people don't understand money. God talks a lot about money and provides many clear instructions on what we are to do with it and how we are to feel about it.

There is a common belief among Christians that money is a bad thing and that if you have a lot of money you must be bad. This is absolutely crazy! In fact, it is practically the opposite. Money is something that God wants us to have. He wants us to live comfortable lives. Think about it. If Christians believe that being rich is bad then who will get rich? The non-Christians. Do you really want the non-Christians to have all the money? I certainly don't!

Money provides the means to accomplish a lot of things, good or evil. If Christians have the majority of the money think of all the good that can be done. However, if non-Christians have all the money think of the things they could do with it. Therefore, it is your duty to learn about money and what God wants you to do with it. You are to be diligent. The Bible says the diligent prosper.

Make it your ambition to increase your wealth in a Godly way. Learn how to handle money God's way and start doing good with the money you have. Money flows from the hands the foolish to the hands of the wise. Remember that a fool and his money are quickly parted. Do you want to be a fool? I hope not. Therefore, become wise with your money. Read this study in addition to your Bible and dedicate the time to learn what God wants you to learn.

This study has been divided up into 14 short lessons that you can read and then discuss with a group of people so that you can all begin to understand money. The lessons are designed to be quick and simple and get you to think. In addition, I encourage you to take the time to reflect on the content and look up the verses mentioned. Really dig deep and examine the scriptures.

Take the effort to educate yourself and discuss this information with those around you. Don't simply read

INTRODUCTION

it and do nothing. Read it and engage with others so you can all help each other out. You will gain much more knowledge by reading the lessons and the accompanying verses and talking about them than if you only read the lessons.

How quickly you move through this devotional is up to you. You can choose to complete one lesson each day and have it done in two weeks or you can use it as an excellent group study topic and complete one lesson each time you meet, which will stretch the course of the study over weeks or months. It is entirely up to you. As long as you take the time to truly understand what is going on then this study will be a success.

Money God's Way

LESSON 1:

HANDLE MONEY GOD'S WAY

Money and possessions are the second most talked-about thing in the Bible. Therefore, they are important. God is spending a lot of time telling you about money, so you need to listen to Him. The Bible is the ultimate financial guide. You need to be wise with your money and listen to what God tells you to do with it. A fool and his money are soon parted; therefore, be wise. God wants you to have a plan for your money. **Be sure you know the condition of your flocks, give careful attention to your herds** (Proverbs 27:23). You probably don't have flocks and herds. However, flocks and herds were assets in Bible times, and you certainly

Money God's Way

have assets. You are to not only know the condition of your assets, but you are to pay careful attention to them. That means you need to know where they are and what they are doing at all times. Your money needs to be budgeted, whether in your mind or on paper, every cent accounted for. Your possessions need to have a place and be well maintained. Nothing is lost. God doesn't lose anything, neither should you. Follow God's plan. He certainly has one.

HANDLE MONEY GOD'S WAY

Money God's Way

LESSON 2:

STEWARDSHIP

Stewardship means to be a steward, and a steward is someone who manages the wealth and assets of another. God calls you to be a good steward, to practice good stewardship. That means that you are a manager of the things you own. You are a steward of the Lord, and everything that you have belongs to Him. He has provided it for you to manage and take care of. You are to manage it wisely and to follow His instructions. That means that the first 10 percent of everything He gives you must go back to God. In addition, everything you have must be used to glorify Him by blessing others. **Each of you should use whatever gift you have received to serve others, as faithful stewards of God's grace in its various forms**

Money God's Way

(1 Peter 4:10). Keep in mind that everything you have belongs to God. You are simply a steward, a manager, of His wealth. If you adopt that mentality, it will also be easier to bless others by giving away your money. It is easier to spend other people's money than your own. Remember that it is all God's and you are to do with it as He commands.

STEWARDSHIP

Money God's Way

LESSON 3:

FIRST 10 PERCENT TO GOD

Honor the LORD with your wealth, with the first fruits of all your crops (Proverbs 3:9). The Bible tells you to give God the first of all your wealth. Although you may not grow crops, you do earn money, and all that money comes from the Lord. But how much do you give Him? Deuteronomy 14:22 says, **Be sure to set aside a tenth of all that your fields produce each year.** You are to give God 10 percent of all your income. This tenth of what you earn is to come off the top of your pay. That means God must be your first payment out of your check. As an example, let's say you make one thousand dollars. You take that cash and give five

Money God's Way

hundred to the mortgage company, two hundred to the grocery store, one hundred to the car dealer, and one hundred to church. You gave one hundred to church, and that is 10 percent, which is good. However, you gave God's 10 percent to the mortgage company. Proverbs 3:9 is very clear that you must give first to God. Then you may do what you please with the rest. There are no exceptions to this. Out of every paycheck, give first to God and then to everyone else.

FIRST 10 PERCENT TO GOD

Money God's Way

LESSON 4:

TITHING TO TEST GOD

You've probably been taught not to test God. Growing up you might have learned of the time when Jesus was tempted and He quoted scripture to the devil to beat the temptations. One of these scriptures was Matthew 4:7, which says, **Jesus answered him, "It is also written: 'Do not put the Lord your God to the test.'"** This scripture was used in reference to an Old Testament passage from Deuteronomy 6:16, which says, **Do not put the LORD your God to the test as you did at Massah.** Both of these show the importance of respecting God's authority and not testing Him. However, in one action, you are permitted to test

Money God's Way

God. In fact, He commands it. **"Test me in this," says the LORD Almighty, "and see if I will not throw open the floodgates of heaven and pour out so much blessing that there will not be room enough to store it"** (Malachi 3:10). Therefore, you are asked directly by God to test Him by bringing your whole tithe to the storehouse. Bring a tenth of your income to your local church and give it back to God; He tells you what will happen if you do this. What are you waiting for?

TITHING TO TEST GOD

LESSON 5:

UNDER A CURSE

You are under a curse—your whole nation—because you are robbing me (Malachi 3:9). God is telling this to His people when discussing the tithe. He told them that they are robbing Him of the tithe, which is to be returned to God. When Adam and Eve were in the garden, they were given one rule. Don't eat of this one tree. They ate of the tree and, as a result, became cursed with the knowledge of good and evil. They now knew right from wrong and were shamed. They took something that wasn't theirs to take, and they placed themselves under a curse. In the same way, when it comes to your income, you have one rule. Tithe the first tenth back to God. **Be sure to set aside a tenth of all that your fields produce each year** (Deuteronomy

14:22). You can choose whether or not you follow this rule. It is really simple. The Bible tells you exactly what to do with the first tenth of your income in Malachi 3:10 **Bring the whole tithe into the storehouse, that there may be food in my house.** That means you must bring it to God's house, your church. Don't keep what's not yours to have.

UNDER A CURSE

Money God's Way

LESSON 6:

ROBBING THE LORD

If you are not tithing, then you are keeping what is not yours to have. You are engaging in the act of greed. According to the Bible, there are only two things you can do with a tithe. You can either bring it back to the Lord (Malachi 3:10). Or you can keep it for yourself and rob God. **"Will a mere mortal rob God? Yet you rob me. But you ask, 'How are we robbing you?' In tithes and offerings"** (Malachi 3:8). The tithe belongs to the Lord. Everything you have belongs to the Lord. God is simply asking you to thank Him for His provisions by returning 10 percent of what He has given you (Deuteronomy 14:22). It is all His anyway, so why not give your tithe back to Him to show your appreciation. If you do, He will reward you (Malachi 3:10). If you don't, then you will be placing yourself under a curse. You will be robbing God, and in so doing, you are robbing yourself of a blessing from God. Therefore, you are placing yourself under a curse (Malachi 3:9). It is your choice. You can be cursed or be blessed. Personally I'd rather be blessed.

ROBBING THE LORD

Money God's Way

LESSON 7:

GIVING IS DIFFERENT THAN TITHING

Giving to those in need is a wonderful way to show your devotion to God. Jesus tells others many times to give to those in need. **Jesus said it is more blessed to give than to receive** (Acts 20:35). However, many people confuse this giving with tithing. People believe that giving and tithing are the same thing. However, they are not. Tithing is to come from the first of your income. This is the first 10 percent of everything you earn (Proverbs 3:9). Giving is done in addition to tithing. It is an additional act of charity done with leftover income. Tithes are to go to your local church, the storehouse (Malachi 3:10). Giving is done to charities, or to those in need. The dynamic and order is something like this: When you receive income, you are to tithe with the first tenth, then you are to pay your bills, then invest and ensure you leave an inheritance for your family (Proverbs 13:22); and then, any other leftover money is yours to do with as you please. You may save it, spend it, or give it. It would be best to practice a combination of the three.

GIVING IS DIFFERENT THAN TITHING

Money God's Way

LESSON 8:

GIVING IN SECRET

In the first part of Matthew 6, there are great instructions on how you are to give to the poor. You are not to announce your giving or to tell others about it (Matthew 6:2). This is something that is between you and God. Your reward will not be from other people, so don't even tell them. The Lord knows exactly what you are giving. Matthew 6:3-4 says, **But when giving to the needy, do not let your left hand know what your right hand is doing, so that your giving may be in secret. Then your Father, who sees what is done in secret, will reward you.** This means tell no one. Do not even let your left hand know what your right hand is doing! Your giving must be done in secret, or you will have no reward from your Father in heaven. This means you must be humble. It's okay if someone sees you, but don't make a spectacle of it. Perform your giving, and if praised by someone, simply be polite and move on. The point is not to intentionally solicit attention and praise for your giving.

GIVING IN SECRET

Money God's Way

LESSON 9:

BE A CHEERFUL GIVER

Each of you should give what you have decided in your heart to give, not reluctantly or under compulsion, for God loves a cheerful giver (2 Corinthians 9:7). God wants you to decide ahead of time what you are going to give. Then He wants you to give it freely and willingly and be cheerful about giving it. You are not to feel obligated; you are to feel privileged. Privileged in that you have the means to give. Remember, giving is different than tithing. Tithing comes off the top of your income and is a fixed amount. Whereas giving comes off the bottom of your income and can vary depending on how much you have. That is why God wants you

Money God's Way

to decide in your heart what you are going to give. If you have money left over this month and decide to put it toward savings, then you are not going to give it away. Maybe you decide to give a certain percentage of your remaining money and then save or spend the rest. Either way, God is telling you to have a plan for your money. God loves plans, and if you want to be like God, then you need to plan as well.

BE A CHEERFUL GIVER

Money God's Way

LESSON 10:

SLAVE TO THE LENDER

The rich rule over the poor, and the borrower is slave to the lender (Proverbs 22:7). If you follow God's plan for your money, then you will learn to hate debt. The borrower is slave to the lender. Do you want to be a slave? I don't think so. Your debt supports the companies to which you are indebted. Your income is becoming outgone and is going to those who are wiser than you. You need to follow God and get out of debt. Think of the good your money could do if it were going where God wants instead of going to those companies. Whoever has will be given more, and they will have an abundance. **Whoever does not**

have, even what they have will be taken from them (Matthew 13:12). Look at how perfectly this applies to the world today. The loan companies that are loaded with money are collecting tons of money from people like you who have nothing compared to them. Money flows from the hands of fools to the hands of the wise. Work to make sure that you are wisely handling your money. Income is yours. You worked hard for your money, why not keep it.

SLAVE TO THE LENDER

Money God's Way

LESSON 11:

OKAY TO BE RICH

Do not be ashamed of becoming wealthy. God wants you to be rich and very well-off. In fact, several of God's followers were very wealthy. Consider Abraham, the father of nations. He was a very rich man who had all kinds of land, livestock, workers, and servants. He was a great follower of God. In addition, Lazarus, the brother of Martha and Mary, was very rich and was a good friend of Jesus. How about Joseph of Arimathea? Of course he was rich. He had a tomb and requested to put Jesus in there after his death. Not only did Joseph place Jesus in his own tomb, but he also prepared the body for burial. This was a very expensive process. All the perfumes and spices that went on a body were very costly. And don't forget Job. Job was arguably

Money God's Way

the most devout follower of God of all time. Job was very blessed and very rich. Then he was literally put through hell by Satan. Yet he still remained faithful to God. Once Satan was through, God blessed Job even more than He blessed him before. God wants to bless you. If you follow Him, you can be very rich indeed.

OKAY TO BE RICH

LESSON 12:

INVEST GOD'S WAY

Money is one of the most widely mentioned topics in the Bible. God spends so much time discussing money because it is very important. In order to go through life on earth, you need money. God wants to provide you with lots of money so you have an enjoyable life on earth (1 Timothy 6:19). You need to follow Him, and He will bless you. He has a foolproof guide for you to follow when it comes to money. He provides you with instructions and wants you to have a plan for your money (Proverbs 13:16). In Ecclesiastes 11:2, He says, **Invest in seven ventures, yes, in eight; you do not know what disaster may come upon the land.** That means you need to invest your money. Not only in long-term investments such as retirement, but also in

Money God's Way

many things. Invest in seven ventures—yes, in eight. God wants you to diversify your money because you do not know what may happen. If you put all your eggs in one basket and the fox comes, you'll be out of eggs. Listen to God, diversify your assets, and be prepared for anything that may happen.

INVEST GOD'S WAY

Money God's Way

LESSON 13:

STORE WEALTH

God wants you to build and store wealth. Proverbs 21:20 says, **The wise store up choice food and olive oil, but fools gulp theirs down.** Not only does God want you to have money, He wants you to save it and use it wisely. This doesn't mean that you are going to store up only earthly treasures (Matthew 6:19). No, you must maintain the focus on your treasures in heaven (Matthew 6:20). However, since you are living on earth, there are earthly things that you must do. One of them is storing money and not becoming obsessed with it. God wants you to store wealth in a godly manner. If you follow His directions for your money, then you will be successful. That means tithing, getting out of debt, storing it, and leaving an

Money God's Way

inheritance. Once that is complete, you can use your money to bless others. You can give it away. When you and your family are taken care of, you can bless others as God blesses you. First Timothy 6:18 says, **Command them to do good, to be rich in good deeds, and to be generous and willing to share.** You know what to do. Build wealth, store an inheritance, and share.

STORE WEALTH

LESSON 14:

LEAVE AN INHERITANCE

A good person leaves an inheritance for their children's children, but a sinner's wealth is stored up for the righteous (Proverbs 13:22). God wants you to store wealth for your family. He wants you to bless others as He blessed you. A good person leaves an inheritance, whereas sinners store wealth for themselves. Do not be so attached to your money like the sinners, it is all God's anyway, and He wants you to have a plan for you money exactly as He has a plan for you. God wants you to provide for your family and take care of them. 1 Timothy 5:8 says, **Anyone who does not provide for their relatives, and especially**

Money God's Way

for their own household, has denied the faith and is worse than an unbeliever. Examine this carefully. Anyone who does not provide for their household is worse than an unbeliever. Your money and wealth is a gift from God. Use it to provide for those around you and leave an inheritance for not only your children, but also your grandchildren. If you follow God's plan for your life, and follow what He says about money, then you will be able to leave that inheritance.

LEAVE AN INHERITANCE

Money God's Way

CONCLUSION

I sincerely hope that you have learned a great deal about money while reading this devotional. I hope that you have changed and improved your way of thinking so that you can start managing your money the way God wants you to manage your money. In addition, I encourage you to share this with everyone you know so that they can start to learn how to manage money as well.

Of course, this isn't going to teach them how to effectively manage money but it is going to teach them how God wants them to behave with money. In addition, it will only do that if they look up and study the verses mentioned. This isn't an all-inclusive study. No, it is a combination of factors that makes it successful. Therefore, if all you did was read through these pages then I strongly advise you to read them again and also read all of the verses mentioned.

Then, take some initiative and start up a small group study and work through these pages with some of your friends. Money is an incredibly important topic. God knows that we live in a fallen world where money is the means to pretty much anything you can think of.

Money God's Way

Therefore, if you can learn how to effectively manage money then you have the power to make some real changes in this world.

It is important that we continue to communicate and discuss the word of God. It is only through studying with other believers that we can really grow. Everyone must have people in their lives that they can study with and talk to.

I look forward to communicating with you.
Spencer Coffman

CONCLUSION

Money God's Way

ABOUT THE AUTHOR

My name is Spencer Coffman. I grew up going to Sunday school and church on a weekly basis. I went through the AWANA program from fourth to sixth grade. AWANA stands for Approved Workmen Are Not Ashamed and is a program that helps kids memorize, and learn about, the Bible. During those years, I memorized over 750 Bible verses and earned the Timothy Award, which is the highest achievement in the elementary AWANA program. After that, I became a leader in AWANA and also participated in High School AWANA clubs. I memorized 750 more verses and earned not only the Meritorious Award but also the Citation. The highest AWANA award.

The church leaders quickly paid attention, and when I was fifteen years old, I was asked to lead an adult study. I did, and the class was a great success. There were twenty or so regular attendees, and together we discussed a variety of controversial topics throughout the Bible. At age sixteen, I enrolled in Alexandria Technical College and no longer led the

Bible study. I then transferred to Minnesota State University Moorhead and conducted a psychological experiment about human behavior and the ability to read emotions. In 2013, one year after graduation, my thesis, Facial Expression: The Ability to Distinguish between Enjoyment and Nonenjoyment Smiles, was published in the Psi Chi Journal of Psychological Research.

I continued to study facial expressions, and in 2015, I wrote and published A Guide to Deception, which is a book that educates readers about deception and teaches them how to detect lies. Currently, I have been working on writing, and publishing, a number of eBooks in addition to publishing 365 Days of Devotion For Everyone.

I'd love to have you visit my website and connect with me on social media. Take a look at my other books and leave some reviews. Share them with your friends and on your social media accounts. It's time the people of God start becoming the people of God. Rise up, and share the Word! To read more about Spencer, visit his website spencercoffman.com

ABOUT THE AUTHOR

Money God's Way

Printed in Great Britain
by Amazon